Assurance Of Salvation

Table of Contents

Track 1- What's Not In The Bible

Do you want to know what's not in the Bible? The Sinner's Prayer.

I believe that there has been such a movement in the church that we have to "Get people saved" that people aren't being saved because they don't know from what they are being saved. Have you ever heard someone say, "Say this prayer and accept Jesus into your heart"? I bet that you have. And sadly, with such a basic approach, we don't get to know who God is and have no idea how much we need Him. And without knowing who God is, we will never have the Assurance of Salvation that we are told to have.

Consider this: Jesus Christ ministered for roughly 3 and a half years to the same 12 people, walking with them, talking with them, sharing the secrets of God with them, and still, Judas Iscariot, one of the 12, betrayed him. My point is that Judas Iscariot walked with Jesus Christ, talked with Jesus Christ, saw miracles done by Jesus Christ and when the devil came, Judas fell.

Nowhere in that 3 and a half years did Jesus say, "Say this prayer and welcome me into your heart." What he did say was, "Follow me."

(I wonder how many of us will fall away because one day we said a prayer with no regard for

God. Don't be surprised that I say this. There are many popular pastors on social media and TV that care very little for the Word and holiness of God.)

Now, I want to point this out: We are blessed, I would argue, more than the disciples of Jesus Christ. Although they walked with him, talked with him, and saw great miracles, Jesus said to them regarding his death that unless he goes, the Holy Spirit will not come (John 16:7). Now, in today's church, we have minimize the Holy Spirit for miracles, speaking in tongues, or healing the sick, which are gifts, but the Holy Spirit is so much more and we need Him more than the miracles. He is the Advocate (John 14:26) to us and He is the Word of God (Bible), but not limited to it. Consider the following,

"The word of God is alive and active. Sharper than any double-edged sword, it penetrates even to dividing soul and spirit, joints and marrow; it judges the thoughts and attitudes of the heart. Nothing in all creation is hidden from God's sight." (Hebrews 4:12-13)

"Take the helmet of salvation and the sword of the Spirit, which is the word of God."
(Ephesians 6:17)

I would like to dedicate this book to my grandparents who, while talking one day, mentioned that it would be great to have "Assurance of Salvation", but concluded that they never would. And to a friend of mine to whom, while we were having coffee one day, I mentioned my spiritual hardships and my lack of "Assurance of Salvation" he commented, "I never knew you had doubts." So I'd like to say that we are meant to have assurance of salvation and it is a blessing of mine to have it.

We will be looking through 2 Peter 1:3-9 on how we ought to live, because it will help us find our assurance:

"Therefore, my brothers and sisters, make every effort to confirm your calling and election. For if you do these things, you will never stumble, and you will receive a rich welcome into the eternal kingdom of our Lord and Savior Jesus Christ."
(2 Peter 1:10-11)

If you are sitting at home reading this, I highly recommend you have a pen and paper handy to take down notes and have a discussion with others. And get out a Bible so you can do your own Bible study. And if you have questions or comments, please contact me and I would love to discuss this further.

Track 2- A Few Verses

One of the things that I did before finishing this book was tell people on a Christian social media website about it. I mentioned the purpose and asked if they had any verses that I may be missing regarding the goal of finding "Assurance of Salvation." And I would like to share the verses they provided. So get your Bible ready as we jump into this.

For God so loved the world that he gave his one and only Son, that whoever believes in him shall not perish but have eternal life. For God did not send his Son into the world to condemn the world, but to save the world through him. (John 3:16-17)

For the wages of sin is death, but the gift of God is eternal life in Jesus Christ our Lord.
(Romans 6:23)

If you declare with your mouth, "Jesus is Lord," and believe in your heart that God raised him from the dead, you will be saved. (Romans 10:9)

And this is the testimony: God has given us eternal life, and this life is in his Son. Whoever has the Son has life; whoever does not have the Son of God does not have life.

I write these things to you who believe in the name of the Son of God so that you may know that you have eternal life. (1 John 5:11-13)

"Whoever acknowledges me (Jesus Christ) before others, I will also acknowledge before my Father in heaven. But whoever disowns me before others, I will disown before my Father in heaven." (Matthew 10:32-33)

These are all great verses, but in this search for assurance, they didn't give me the soul satisfying guarantee that I am eternally saved. Because Matthew 7:21-23 says that even people who, in the name of Jesus Christ, will prophesy and do great miracles will not enter the kingdom of Heaven. So my search was still on.

"If you love me, keep my commandments. And I will ask the Father, and he will give you another advocate to help you and be with you forever…" (John 14:15-16)

Now, we can't "love" through simple obedience. However, it is through knowing that the commandments are good, that we learn to love the one who gave them.

Does that make sense to you? There was a draw, an attraction, to your sin. Adam and Eve were drawn to the fruit on the Tree of Knowledge of Good and Evil in the Garden of Eden. It wasn't until afterwards that they realized the true price of their sin. And, no, it wasn't the banishment from the Garden of Eden, it was the shame.

It's hard to understand this concept of "love" for a commandment, but I will try to explain further. I'm going to tell you now to recognize that God loves you and wants you to live in communion with Him and others.

One vitally important thing that I do want to say is this: I don't know when someone is "saved". I think when we step into eternal life we will be surprised at who we find there. Apostle Paul quotes Exodus and says that "God will have mercy on whom he will have mercy…" so it's not for me to decide. Apostle Paul also tells the Philippian church to "work out your salvation with fear and trembling." While I would like to remind you of the well known verse John 3:16, I would like to share John 3:19-20 which is a call on us who claim Jesus Christ as Lord.

This is the verdict: Light has come into the world, but people loved darkness instead of light because their deeds were evil. Everyone who does evil hates the light, and will not come into the light for fear that their deeds will be exposed. (John 3:19-20)

Track 3- The Wholeness Of A Holy God

In the previous chapter, I shared a number of verses that say belief in Jesus Christ is all the "assurance" we need. But who is Jesus Christ? If we don't know who he is, how can we "believe" in him?

(There is a number of scripture that there is a false gospel message of Jesus Christ. Jesus warns in Matthew 24:4-5 about deception of people coming in his name. Apostle Paul shares how astonished he is that people have left the true gospel for a false one in Galatians 1:6-9. In 2 Corinthians 11, Paul warns against false teachers saying that, "Satan himself masquerades as an angel of light." Among many other verses where the message of Jesus Christ is brought forth by false prophets and apostles, and the message of salvation has become a message of finances (1 Timothy 6).)

I want to share with you the truth of God, I call it "The Wholeness of a Holy God".

Jesus Christ is NOT separate from the God of the Old Testament. The God who brought the Israelites out of Egypt and led them as they wandered the desert for 40 years is the same one Jesus glorifies. And Jesus lived his life whole life in obedience to the same God that gave the Israelites the law. Even at the time of his death, Jesus was obedient ("Not my will, but yours be done") in the completion of the Sacrificial Law that God gave in the book of Leviticus.

You need to know this because a simple 'confession' of Jesus Christ should not be your assurance alone.

Now, the question is, 'How can the loving Jesus Christ be equal to the angry God of the Old Testament, who talked about stoning women for adultery or killing children for walking away from the faith?'

Jesus Christ is the embodiment of those laws and shows us the mercy of God. The example of when the Pharisees catch a woman in adultery comes to mind. The Pharisees bring her to Jesus and say, "According to the law of Moses we are to stone such a woman." (This is a selective passage from Deuteronomy 22.) And Jesus says, "You who are without sin cast the first stone." And all the men walked away because they knew that they were all guilty of sin and had no right to stone her. Now, Jesus, being God in the flesh, was the only one lawfully able to stone that woman, but he said to her, "Neither do I condemn you."

(Jesus also said, "Go now and leave your life of sin" which will be brought up in a future chapter. You can read the full account in John 8:4-11.)

Jesus Christ is showing the same mercy of God in the Old Testament. Mercy shown, not because of sacrificed animals, but because in God's very nature, is merciful.

Now, I recommend people read the books Exodus, Leviticus and Deuteronomy to get a better picture of who God is, but I'll share it now. God's Law which is "holy, righteous and good," is what separates us Christians from the rest of the world. The nations around the Israelites had idol prostitutes, which God condemns: Nations offered their children in fire, they had sexual relations with animals, men would have sexual relations with their own mothers, sisters, aunts, daughters, sisters-in-law, daughters-in-law, step-mothers, step-daughters, and offered their children as prostitutes to their 'gods'. You can read Leviticus 18 where God says that it is the nations around them that do these sexual things.

You'll notice that I didn't mention Leviticus 18:22 which says not to lie with a man as you would with a woman. People like to say, "Well, that's Old Testament law and is irrelevant," which is countered by sharing New Testament verses (1 Cor. 5:11; 1 Cor. 6:9; 1 Tim. 1:10; Jude 1:7).

I left this out because today it is used as a political talking point and nothing more. I felt the need to address this topic in detail because the human soul is far too valuable to be swept aside because of discomfort:

1. Homosexual sin is not a worse off sexual sin than the rest. Leviticus 18 shares a long list of sexual sins, all condemned before God. James 2:10 tells us that if we are guilty of committing one sin, we're guilty of breaking them all.

   In 1 Corinthians 5, Apostle Paul addresses a specific sexual sin and says, "...even pagans do not tolerate: A man is sleeping with his father's wife."

2. In 1 Timothy 1:10, Apostle Paul, regarding the law, says that it was made for lawbreakers and rebels, including "those practicing homosexuality."

   I wanted to share this for those who genuinely want God and the eternal life that you were created for. Paul's word usage gives great hope that you are not "a homosexual" as the world defines you, but that you are a sinner just like the rest of humanity fully dependant on God's grace.

I want to tell you that all of these laws are to keep the nation of Israel holy. And we are saved, not by our perfect obedience to the law, but because of the mercy of Jesus Christ. And when God says, "Don't do something," it's not because he is trying to make rules, but because of his love for us.

I can testify to the goodness of godly living, putting away foolishness for the sake of holiness. Of course, I'm not perfect, but my eternal hope and faith is founded in the grace of God shown to me on the cross.

Perhaps we don't have the religions that God spoke against in the time of Moses, but we are still to be separated as a holy people. We still have fortune tellers and spiritists, we are still in a time where sexual promiscuity is everywhere, we have drunkards and prostitutes, and we have foul language coming out of our mouths. The tongue, James 3 says, is like a small rudder steering a large ship.

So, "belief" in Jesus Christ is not just believe and then go on and live your life. It is an acknowledgement of the goodness of God, living your life seeking him, through his Word for counsel, and accepting that it took another to make you perfect before him.

Track 4- Knowledge

The friend that I had coffee with has been my friend for at least 10 years. Although we don't see each other as much as we'd like, we have kept our friendship going for a long time through a mutual love of the famous Rocky Balboa movies starring Sylvester Stallone. And this friend of mine knows some of the things that I've done in my past, things I wish I had never done, things of which I'm ashamed. However, this friend of mine works in a prison and he has seen the worst of the worst so what I shared with him seems quite innocent in comparison.

Now, for those who don't know, I am married. I was married in July 2018. My wife and I go see my grandparents every few weeks and my grandmother has said on a number of those visits that I did it (referring to getting married) in a good way. Commenting I didn't rush into marriage, and I took my time and I waited.

I argue that there is nothing good about me. Nothing good about the steps I took into getting married. And, if given the chance, I would speak against everything that I had done in that process. And although my friend has seen men who have done "the worst", it does not make me "good".

So today's verse comes from Hosea 4:6 where God says,

"…my people are destroyed for their lack of knowledge. Because you have rejected knowledge, I also reject you… because you have ignored the law of your God, I also will ignore your children."

For those who don't know, Hosea was a prophet of God. In the book of Hosea, God calls Hosea to marry a promiscuous, prostitute woman. So Hosea marries a woman named Gomer. After they have a couple children, Gomer goes back to being a promiscuous woman. In Hosea 3:1, it says, The LORD said to me (Hosea), "Go, show your love to your wife again, though she is loved by another man and is an adulteress. Love her as the LORD loves the Israelites…" And verse 2, Hosea has to buy back his wife.

My point as to why Hosea is so relevant is because we are all like that adulterous woman. We have all gone our own way. And as we seek our "Assurance of Salvation", it's interesting how God so often associates his Law to the salvation of his people. In Hosea 4:6 says, "Because you have rejected knowledge, I also reject you… because you have ignored the law of your God, I also will ignore your children."

My wife and I discuss the topic of the Law in regards to the message of Jesus Christ. I point out that Jesus Christ wasn't born to a woman in Scotland, Ireland, Canada, or America (even if they were established countries at the time). He was born to a people under the Law of God, and to a people who were condemned by the religious leaders who were obedient to that Law, but denied the mercy and grace of God.

Like I say, so many people have faith in Jesus Christ, but don't act in any of the ways he did which was in accordance with the Old Testament Law. We don't change the way we act, we don't change the way we associate with people, and we don't change the way we speak. Remember that Jesus Christ said that he did not come to abolish the Law, but to fulfill it.

In this book, I'm not going to go deep into the topic of the Law- what laws are ceremonial that we aren't under, which laws are sacrificial which Jesus Christ's death and resurrection completed and which Law is "good, holy and just" as Apostle Paul says in Romans 7:12.

The question is concerning knowledge. God says, concerning his people Israel, "my people are destroyed for their lack of knowledge."

My friend who works in prison thinks it's ironic that public schools no longer encourage reading the Bible, but that it is encouraged reading material in prison. I wonder how things would have changed for those prisoners if they had the knowledge of scripture. Would they even be in prison?

And for those who think it is "good" that I married when I was 30. I would encourage anyone reading this to hear my counsel that marriage is a beautiful thing, but the more you date and sleep around trying to find "the one", you're fooling yourself. There is nothing good about me. It was in my surrender to God and shutting off all the noise of this world (literally shutting off the TV shows where sexual promiscuity is glorified) that I could reach the emotional and mental maturity for marriage.

My main point in life is that we may know that God is good and that He loves us. But if we believe that God is good, why do we so easily disregard His Laws by misunderstanding Apostle Paul and say, "We are no longer under law, but grace."

Consider this: A man may leave his wife and children for a time to fight in a war. A man, who is forced away by circumstance, still loves his children, and still sends home letters filled with wisdom and counsel to his wife and children. However, there are other men who have children, live in the same city, maybe even the same house, and are in every way an absent, useless father.

Who do you think loves his children more?

That's how I picture my God, who, for the time is physically absent, but I know he loves me because of his counsel.

If you would like to do a little Bible reading, go to Leviticus 19 and consider those laws. Consider, "How is God showing his love with these laws?" In Leviticus 19, you will see some of the laws focus on the specific times while others are still relevant today. I bring this up because many people believe that the Old Testament laws are all irrelevant and oppressive and that's foolish.

Finally, in your quest for assurance read what 2 Peter 1:5-9 says,

"For this very reason, make every effort to add to your faith goodness; and to goodness, knowledge; and to knowledge, self-control; and to self-control, perseverance; and to perseverance, godliness; and to godliness, mutual affection; and to mutual affection, love. For if you possess these qualities in increasing measure, they will keep you from being ineffective and unproductive in your knowledge of our Lord Jesus Christ. But whoever does not have them is nearsighted and blind, forgetting that they have been cleansed from their past sins."

Track 5- Repentance

I think the idea of repentance is hard to understand as there is a true and false repentance. The man on the cross who died next to Jesus said, "Remember me when you come into your kingdom." And Jesus replied, "Today you'll be in paradise." (Luke 23:42-43) This is what many believe, but it's not the whole story. Consider what Peter said regarding increasing in godliness, knowledge, perseverance, etc. The man on the cross, of course, had no time to increase in anything; he was judged and condemned by the law, likely a law that we would give people a slap on the wrist today for committing.

My point in bringing this up is that we are judged by God's law. We shouldn't watch the 6 o'clock news and think we are "good". We should look at Jesus Christ for our standard of good.

I don't know when true repentance happens. I don't know if when Jesus called out Peter and Andrew on the boat and said, "Come follow me," if they were eternally saved at that moment. Peter says in 2 Peter 1:5, "...add to your faith, goodness; and to goodness, knowledge..." Peter walked with Jesus for three and a half years and still messed up: Years after Jesus died, rose again and ascended to Heaven, Apostle Paul had to confront Peter regarding his approach to favouring the Jewish people and the traditional laws they followed over the Gentiles who had no religious or cultural law, but believed and were saved by the same Jesus Christ that Peter knew (Galatians 2:11-21). And, as James points out, favouritism is a sin (James 2:1-13).

My point is that I don't know when you are officially saved, only God does. But I do believe in prayer, and studying scripture, and obeying the Word and one day a light just clicks and you go from a religious attitude of "Oh no, I can't do that or God will smite me" to a "Oh My… God loves me, he wants the best for me and all this time I have foolishly been trying to find my own satisfaction in life."

I think I came to this point when I was about to get married, prior to asking her. I realized that not everyone "deserves" to be married, me most of all. I don't deserve to get married. It's a covenant between man, woman, and God, the covenant which I have broken. But the same grace that God gives me to love my wife despite my past is the same grace that Christ gives me to go before my Heavenly Father in prayer, worship and studying His words. Sadly, of course, most people don't see marriage that way and God has been kicked out of it. And we wonder why divorce rates are so high.

Now, if you get to this point of repentance, where the guilt of your past sins begins to flood you and you can't move forward with your life consider it good. As my sins hold unto me, let's read Hebrews 4:6-7;

Therefore since it still remains for some to enter that rest, and since those who formerly had the good news proclaimed to them did not go in because of their disobedience, God again set a certain day, calling it "Today." This he did when… he spoke through David, as in the passage already quoted:

"Today, if you hear his voice,
do not harden your hearts."

You may have heard scripture; you may know the Bible, but still not "enter that rest." Of course, allow me to share the context, that this is written to the Jewish religious people who had heard the message of Jesus Christ. And even though they heard of Jesus Christ and believed in his message, they continued to make their religious sacrifices and didn't have faith that only he can take away sin.

But I believe this also applies to us. I grew up in the church. I knew the Bible. I knew right from wrong. But I perverted God's grace as a permission to sin. The verses above share that others too had the message preached to them, but they too never entered the rest because of their disobedience.

When true repentance happens, which is different than simply believing in Jesus Christ's death on the cross and resurrection from the dead, you will find your assurance. This is why I have to correct people when they say that I am "good."

Now, the question for me personally is, Should I confront people of sins? Matthew 18:15 tells us, "If your brother or sister sins, go and point out their fault, just between the two of you. If they listen to you, you have won them over." But it's hard because John 1:14, we are told that Jesus was full of "grace and truth." So I don't want to judge people for their sins, but counsel them, which, I believe, shows both "grace and truth."

I don't think we should 'confront' people of their sins as if listing off complaints against them. I believe we all fall away from God's perfect Law, such as King David who slept with another man's wife, and killed her husband to hide his shame, didn't recognize his sins. It took a prophet named Nathan to confront David about his actions for him to notice them as sin.

So today, I want to ask you something... If I came to you and said, "Hey, I don't think that thing you did (maybe it's favouring someone, maybe it's a show you watch, maybe it's the manner in which you speak which is disrespectful) is the way God wants," would you be offended? Or would you say, "Show me in scripture", and allow God to speak over you? Or, as I mentioned regarding the 6 O'clock news, would you consider yourself "good" by that standard?

My point is that if I simply listed off your sins that I see on a daily basis, it means nothing. You can apologize, but it doesn't mean the Holy Spirit is working in you. Jesus says in John 3 that one must be 'born again' by the Holy Spirit to enter the kingdom of Heaven. So the question is not, "Are you sorry for your sins?" The question is, "Do you love God? Do you believe that God is good?" Because if you love God, when I, or someone else reveals to you about a past or potentially future sin, your repentance will be genuine.

When David was confronted by Nathan about his sin that he failed to recognize, he didn't defend himself by judging others, he said in 2 Samuel 12:13, "I have sinned against the LORD." And David went on to write Psalm 51, which I encourage you to read, and in verse 12 David says, "Restore unto me the joy of your salvation."

So, do you find joy in God? If I confront you of a sin, will you welcome it?

Track 6- The Holy Spirit

The Holy Spirit has become so complex through scripture. Mainly because we believe that evidence of the Holy Spirit is through the gifts such as speaking in the tongues of angels, or having dreams and visions, or healing the sick and raising the dead. But Jesus shows that there is a difference between gifts and fruits in Matthew 7.

> "Not everyone who says to me, 'Lord, Lord,' will enter the kingdom of heaven, but only the one who does the will of my Father who is in heaven. Many will say to me on that day, 'Lord, Lord, did we not prophesy in your name and in your name drive out demons and in your name perform many miracles?' Then I will tell them plainly, 'I never knew you. Away from me, you evildoers!' (Matthew 7:21-23)

So people will list the spiritual gifts they have, but Jesus will not recognize them. They are unsaved. But he says that by a person's fruit you will recognize the true and false prophets or teachers. I believe that applies to us all.

> "Watch out for false prophets. They come to you in sheep's clothing, but inwardly they are ferocious wolves. By their fruit you will recognize them."
> (Matthew 7:15-16)

Now the word 'fruits' refers to how you live your life. Maybe on Sunday you go to church, read scripture, speak in tongues, sing in the choir, but what of the rest of your life? Outside of the church you are listening to trashy music, watching trashy shows, having extra-marital relationships, swearing, dishonouring your parents, seeking fortune tellers and spiritists, etc. To this Jesus will say, "Away from me, you evildoers!"

So today, let's look at the 'Fruits of the Spirit'.

So I say, walk by the Spirit, and you will not gratify the desires of the flesh. For the flesh desires what is contrary to the Spirit, and the Spirit what is contrary to the flesh. They are in conflict with each other, so that you are not to do whatever you want. But if you are led by the Spirit, you are not under the law.

The acts of the flesh are obvious: sexual immorality, impurity and debauchery; idolatry and witchcraft; hatred, discord, jealousy, fits of rage, selfish ambition, dissensions, factions and envy; drunkenness, orgies, and the like. I warn you, as I did before, that those who live like this will not inherit the kingdom of God.

But the fruit of the Spirit is love, joy, peace, forbearance, kindness, goodness, faithfulness, gentleness and self-control.

Against such things there is no law. Those who belong to Christ Jesus have crucified the flesh with its passions and desires. Since we live by the Spirit, let us keep in step with the Spirit. Let us not become conceited, provoking and envying each other. (Galatians 5:16-26)

Galatians 5:23, after listing the fruits of the Spirit says, "Against such things there is no law." You don't have to be 'under the law' to love others. You don't have to be 'under the law' to be joyful, to be peaceful, to be gentle. That's the true Spirit of the Law.

So, today's discussion is to re-read the verses provided from Galatians 5:16-26 and think about areas in your life where you can improve. If you believe God loves you and that He is good, you can realize your short comings and pray to Jesus Christ to forgive you of your sins.

We know that there are wicked people in the world, and we say, "I'm glad that I'm nothing like that person who shot kids in school, or a rapist, or whatever." But Jesus said in the famous Sermon on the Mount that if you look at someone with sexual thoughts, you're an adulterer/rapist (Matthew 5:27-30). And anyone who calls someone a fool is a murderer and "in danger of the fire of Hell" (Matthew 5:21-22). So to my grandparents and my coffee friend or anyone else listening, that's the standard to which I hold myself. This is the standard that we should all hold ourselves.

It is impossible to live to the standard of perfection that God calls us to live. I repeat: impossible. If we read scripture and try to "live by the law" we will fail. The only way is to love the God who gave the law.

Does that make sense?

Imagine it this way: Can you manage to stay married to your spouse if you don't love him or her? Can you, every day, wake up, see the same person, day after day, watch the same shows and movies that person likes, eat the same food, and on and on?

I doubt it.

Now, if you are willing to accept such a high standard of living, how are you going to do it?

"When an impure spirit comes out of a person, it goes through arid places seeking rest and does not find it. Then it says, 'I will return to the house I left.' When it arrives, it finds the house unoccupied, swept clean and put in order. Then it goes and takes with it seven other spirits more wicked than itself, and they go in and live there. And the final condition of that person is worse than the first. That is how it will be with this wicked generation." (Matthew 12:43-45)

First off, as I said before, I don't know at what time you are 'saved'. This book is for those seeking assurance. Some are "saved" when they do something horrible and are immediately realizing the consequences. That's why I've heard it said that a lot of people find God in prison. Some grow up in the church and know The Ten Commandments, but still fall away, because they don't understand the benefits of God. And that's where I come in.

I began going to church and believed in Jesus Christ when I was 5 or 6 years old through a children's program. However, I would argue that I wasn't "saved" until I was 27 and couldn't find assurance until I was 30. And I found that assurance through reading scripture and prayer and recognizing how bad I truly am by realizing how good God truly is.

I grew up in church with the mentality of, "Oh no. I can't do this or God will punish me." But, after living a life trying to find a wife and satisfaction, I realized that only God can satisfy me and I needed to find out who God is.

Matthew 12:43-45 tells us that it's one thing to clean up your life and live a "good" life, but when trials come, you will be left off worse than you began. I testify that it was impossible for me to overcome my addictions without the Holy Spirit, which is, in part, the Word of God (Ephesians 6:17). So, like what Jesus says, if you simply cleaned up, what's stopping more spirits, desires and temptations, from re-entering you?

So I turned my life around, I cleaned up, I dedicated to writing Christian books and to the study and to the advancement of God's kingdom. And after writing God: The Master of Sin and Satan the Beautiful, I was baptized. And, I believe, that the Holy Spirit filled me from that time (not because of a supernatural work of water, but one of obedience). Addictions I had were being removed, mostly from turning off the TV and God filled those places with reading scripture. For three years after my baptism, my life was filled with so much doubt and fear over this quest to find my "Assurance of Salvation." But, as frightening as it was, I'm glad I went through it because it brings me to a place where I can counsel others.

Again, I recommend you read Exodus, Leviticus, and Deuteronomy and be reminded about the holiness that God desires for his people. Whether you live in America, Canada, Mexico, Britain, wherever, we are all welcomed into the house of God. And Jesus Christ desires no different holy living than God the Father did in the Old Testament.

So today's homework is to Be Holy and Have a Humble Heart. One thing that is noticeable in the books Exodus, Leviticus and Deuteronomy is this teaching of "Be Holy as I (God) am holy" or "I am the LORD your God who makes you holy." This is a hard concept to follow knowing that you will never be able to be perfect but that you are to aim for such holy perfection. And if you do read the books mentioned and again and again recognize your sins, it means your heart is being humbled and you are taking responsibility for those sins. Then say, "Thank God for Jesus Christ who washes away my sins." And then have a heart to forgive others of their misdeeds against you.

Today's Prayer: When Nathan confronted King David about his sins regarding sleeping with another man's wife and killing her husband, David wrote Psalm 51. In Psalm 51:11, he says, "Do not cast me from your presence or take your Holy Spirit from me."

David wasn't afraid that, "Oh no. God is going to condemn me to Hell for sure." He knew that God loved him. He knew that God was good. The problem was that he didn't recognize his sins and it took, what I believe, over 9 months for him to recognize his sin. It was when the prophet, Nathan, confronted him that he realized that something was missing: The Holy Spirit. So that was his prayer.

So today, if you recognize God as the eternal God, the holy God, who is from everlasting to everlasting, believe that his Law is 'holy, righteous and good', pray for the Holy Spirit. Jesus says in Luke 11:13 that "your Father in Heaven will give the Holy Spirit to those who ask Him."

So, with a humble heart, tell your prayer to God and ask God to convict you of your sins. And when He does, don't be afraid, say, "Thank God for Jesus Christ," and turn away from your sins.

Track 8- Grow In Love

When I first met my wife's pastor prior to us getting married, he asked me, "Do I love her?" I didn't have an answer. Even when we got married, I don't know if I "love" her the same as her pastor loves his wife of 30 years. Love is this supernatural complex thing. Love in not like Hollywood portrays love in a romantic comedy. Love, the way God tells us to love, is unnatural, it is unselfish, it is sacrificial.

About a month after getting married, my wife had back surgery and I had to help her do a lot of things. I won't give details, but my point is that the "romance" in the comedy of my life was not there. But I still love my wife and I grow to love her. This makes me sound like I've been married for 50 years or something, but my point is about what love truly is. And it's not the selfish love of Hollywood.

Ephesians 5:25 and 32 says, "Husbands, love your wives as Christ loved the church and gave himself up for her... This is a profound mystery- but I'm talking about Christ and the church."

Now, I'm not giving marriage advice here. And neither is Apostle Paul. He is using marriage to illustrate this sacrificial love.

"Whoever does not love does not know God, because God is love." (1 John 4:8)

It's hard to find "Assurance of Salvation" when we are driven by fear. I testify to how hard it is. "Oh no, I watched this movie and they swore, will God forgive me for watching it? Am I going to Hell because of it?"

You can't grow to love God with that mentality. In the same way you can't grow to love your wife or your parents or friends with that mentality. It's not love, it's fear.

Consider these steps for growing in a marriage relationship:
1. Man meets woman.
2. Man gets to know woman.
3. Man marries woman.
4. Man lives with woman and continues dialogue and getting to know woman.

I'm sure that you could add more steps to this list, but I'm simply trying to prove a point. The problem that I want to point out today is that the approach many have with God is wrong. Here is the step:
1. Say this prayer and ask Jesus into your heart.

It's a short list. There is no growth. There s no knowledge, which 2 Peter 1:5 tells us is a vital step to love. And there is absolutely no desire to know Him.

Now, let's try applying the same steps with God as we do in the relationship between a man and woman:

1. Man meets God (maybe at church, hears about God through a friend, etc)
2. Man gets to know God (attends church, listens to pastors, asks questions and gets answers from others who know Him, read the Bible, etc. Thus, he gains knowledge)
3. Man "marries" God (you make a decision to be in unity with God)
4. Man lives with God and continues dialogue and getting to know God (you live with God, not just church on Sundays, you read the Bible, you seek the Bible for counsel, you pray, you grow in knowledge)

Now, this booklet is about finding "Assurance of Salvation" and you might be thinking, "Oh no. I don't have enough time to 'grow' in this relationship." Maybe you need to start with the man on the cross next to Jesus who had even less time than you. He said, "Remember me." And Jesus said, "You got it." But, from there, what will you do?

I fear that a lot of people don't know God and if they have assurance, it may be in vain.

Maybe you reading this is your first step, like the man on the cross who feared God and asks Jesus to remember him. The man on the cross knew he did something that warranted such punishment, but do you? I doubt that the man on the cross, if taken off of that cross, would commit the same crime that put him there.

In the previous chapter, I encouraged you to pray for the Holy Spirit to work in you. Pray that you believe in the goodness of God and ask him to convict you of your sins. King David, who loved God and believed that God was good and wholly satisfying, said,

"...who can discern their own errors?
Forgive my hidden faults.
Keep your servant also from willful sins;
may they not rule over me.
Then I will be blameless,
innocent of great transgression." (Psalm 19:12-13)

Track 9- Spiritual Maturity and Righteous Living

I want to tell you that applying the scripture to your daily life is what matters. James 2:24 tells us that "a person is considered righteous by what they do and not by faith alone." So today's topic is on spiritual maturity and righteous living.

"You need milk, not solid food! Anyone who lives on milk, being still an infant, is not acquainted with the teaching about righteousness. But solid food is for the mature, who by constant use have trained themselves to distinguish good from evil." (Hebrews 5:12-14)

"Therefore, rid yourselves of all malice and all deceit, hypocrisy, envy, and slander of every kind. Like newborn babies, crave pure spiritual milk, so that by it you may grow up in your salvation, now that you have tasted that the Lord is good." (1 Peter 2:1-3)

Peter says that you can 'grow up in your salvation' after 'you have tasted that the Lord is good.' I think that your assurance will also grow the more you realize that 'the Lord is good'.

I've heard it said that salvation simply comes from a miraculous one time occasion. However, Psalm 34:8 says, "Taste and see that the LORD is good." First we must taste, and then we see. It's like how my pastor always reminds me to look back and see how far God has brought me.

I want to discuss Hebrew 5:14 regarding the distinguishing good from evil. As I've said, we distinguish good from evil by the 6 o'clock news. It's easy to watch and say, "This is good and this is evil." But I think scripture reminds me of constant improvements I can make and it's hard to recognize my own 'good and evil'. This book has been about finding "Assurance of Salvation." Peter tells us in both 1 Peter 1:3-11 and 2 Peter 2:1-3 that we are to continue growing in knowledge.

On the topic of righteous living, I would recommend reading Colossians 3. The following is a section from that chapter.

Since, then, you have been raised with Christ, set your hearts on things above, where Christ is, seated at the right hand of God. Set your minds on things above, not on earthly things.

Put to death, therefore, whatever belongs to your earthly nature: sexual immorality, impurity, lust, evil desires and greed, which is idolatry. Because of these, the wrath of God is coming. You used to walk in these ways, in the life you once lived. But now you must also rid yourselves of all such things as these: anger, rage, malice, slander, and filthy language from your lips. Do not lie to each other, since you have taken off your old self with its practices and have put on the new self, which is being renewed in knowledge in the image of its Creator.

Therefore, as God's chosen people, holy and dearly loved, clothe yourselves with compassion, kindness, humility, gentleness and patience. Bear with each other and forgive one another if any of you has a grievance against someone. Forgive as the Lord forgave you. And over all these virtues put on love, which binds them all together in perfect unity.

Let the peace of Christ rule in your hearts, since as members of one body you were called to peace. And be thankful. Let the message of Christ dwell among you richly as you teach and admonish one another with all wisdom through psalms, hymns, and songs from the Spirit, singing to God with gratitude in your hearts. (Colossians 3:1-2, 5-10, 12-16)

Again, I don't know when someone is saved. As James 2:24 tells us, it's not just about faith alone, but by what we do with it. Using the hard words of Paul, let us "put to death" these old passions and desires: Sexual thoughts, porn, the love of money and possessions which is greed.

I wish churches taught on these verses. True faith is not simply believing in Jesus Christ, and using him as a steppingstone for your best life now, but believing in his message. Jesus Christ freed me from so much. And with those former passions gone, I get to work on the other things such as anger, rage, malice, slander, and foul language. And we are to clothe ourselves with compassion, kindness, humility, gentleness and patience. And "Let the peace of Christ rule in your hearts…"

None of us will be perfect, but by the grace of God, we don't have to be. Sadly, I fear that too often we get comfortable in that "grace" and don't seek out the true joy of God.

My wife knows that I struggle. I struggle with my anger and my language when frustrated. And I realize how harmful these things are to me and my relationships with others. So I seek God to calm my spirit.

My friend who works in prison hears all sorts of language from the inmates. He has told me that some of the guards he works with use the same language back at the inmates. How foolish is that? That's quite literally drinking the same poison. Jesus tells us that what goes into the body doesn't make us unclean, but what comes out of the mouth because it comes from the heart.

So, today's prayer is on dealing with this hardness of heart: Dealing with foul language, dealing with a constant hunger for more money and possessions which is greed or dealing with sexual addictions and habits.

Faith and prayer are great, but as James 2:24 says, they need to be accompanied by action. In the next chapter, I will share my story and steps I took to overcome the same habits that Paul addresses.

Track 10- My Story

Last night I had a dream about a beach. And while I was lying in bed trying to figure out where I had seen this beach before, it made me think of my past and my sins. And as much as I don't want to be reminded of my past, I think that's how God works sometimes: Although God forgives us of our sins, when we remember it, we need to remember that we are saved by Jesus Christ and no other.

I don't much want to share "My Story" because two of the people I'm writing this book for are my grandparents. But I prayed to God to use my sins to bring people to Him and to a true repentance. So here we go.

Now, we live in a hyper-sexualized culture. Pornography is available all over the place and TV shows and movies that are now so common would have been rated R years ago. And I fell into that culture. Before pornography was on every cell phone, it was on the computer, and before that, it was in printed magazines.

This is why I hate when I'm used as an example of "goodness" because I am reminded daily of how I am not. God is my standard of goodness.

So my story begins with me being this good little Christian boy who goes to church and tries to "get people saved" through faith in Jesus Christ. And, so what if I had an addiction to pornography throughout my teen years, Jesus will forgive me of my sins, right?

That's what I was taught in church: Do whatever you want, and Jesus will forgive you and you will go to Heaven. So why stop looking at pornography, right? Why stop getting drunk every night? Why stop treating people poorly? Why stop lying? Why stop taking advantage of people's emotions and finances? Jesus will take me to Heaven when I die, and all will be forgiven.

This is why I talk about a true repentance and a false repentance. A true repentance comes from a genuine recognition of sin and acknowledging God and godly living as something better. I don't believe a saviour is simply one to save us from the wrath of God, but to show us a new way to live. Because Jesus prayed in John 17: 3, "Now this is eternal life: that they know you, the only true God…" If God is only known as a God of wrath, why would Jesus pray that we may know him?

Maybe your sins and addictions are not sexual related. Jesus confronted Pharisees on many occasions concerning a number of sins. Consider reading Matthew 23:13-39 where Jesus pours into the Pharisees and the teachers of the law for their sins. Jesus says to do as they say, but not as they do.

For those who think their porn use is "innocent" and not hurting anyone, Jesus says it's a sin. And he doesn't say things are sinful to deny you pleasure, but to save you from hurt. One reason it's a sin is that we are not created to be alone in our bedroom with a computer screen: Sex is about intimacy, not isolation. Today we know that there is an increasing rise of depression and anxiety and isolation as there is also a rise in porn use.

> Flee from sexual immorality. All other sins a person commits are outside the body, but whoever sins sexually, sins against their own body. (1 Corinthians 6:18)

My point to all of this is to testify that there is freedom in Christ. And that freedom doesn't come through a sense of, "Oh no, I did it again, please forgive me." It is like Psalm 34:8 says about tasting and seeing that the LORD is good.

So, if you have a porn or sexual addiction that you are struggling with, don't simply pray for it to leave. Take active steps to go along with your prayer. I got rid of my online dating accounts, turned off the TV and became very selective about the movies I watched. But I also had to fill that empty spot with actions that are God glorifying.

I remember praying on my knees at the side of my bed and say, "Lord. I know what I want, but you don't want me to do that. Either you take this from me or I will die on my knees." And I would fall asleep many times on my knees.

Consider the following:

"The Lord is with you when you are with him. If you seek him, he will be found by you, but if you forsake him, he will forsake you." (2 Chronicles 15:2)

The verse above is from prophet Azariah to Asa, King of Judah. I think that the prophet's words and the king's actions can be related to all of us. After hearing what the prophet said, King Asa removed the detestable idols from the towns of Judah. You can read this account in 2 Chronicles 15.

Now, for many of us, we don't have physical idols in our homes to be destroyed. But as we read in Colossians 3, greed, which is a constant desire for more, is idolatry. I testify that tithing a regular 10% to my church consistently freed me from financial "idolatry". It freed me from this hunger for more money. And in my soul, I was freed from judging myself for how little I had in comparison to others.

Other "idols" such as pride were removed by me accepting my place in this world. I stopped seeking to be better than others in the church. Instead, I sought out God and realized that He may not want me to be the pastor; maybe God wants me to humble myself. And as my pastor of my new church asks me to take a "leadership" position I am greatly concerned because of my pride.

Pride isn't just about gloating about what you have. You can be prideful in your poverty: "Oh. I have so little. You don't know what it's like to be so poor." You can be prideful in your humility, which is somewhat of an opposite, considering humility is looking less at yourself and pride is looking at yourself as better than others. But an example of being prideful in your humility is gloating about how sacrificial you are: "I wish I could purchase that, but I just gave all my money to this homeless person." Jesus says to not let your left hand know what your right hand is doing. I believe this is to avoid this sense of pride.

There are so many other things in our lives that can hold onto us. Consider favouring people: God says in Exodus 23 not to show favoritism in law suits. Paul speaks against favouritism in the church. This is hard because people naturally gravitate towards people of identical interests. If I plan on going golfing, I contact people who like golfing. If I'm going to go fishing, I contact people who like to fish. Maybe this is common sense to invite people who wish to come, but what about when people new to the church community are trying to fit in? Or what about favouring people within a family?

If you show special attention to the man wearing fine clothes and say, "Here's a good seat for you," but say to the poor man, "You stand there" or "Sit on the floor by my feet," have you not discriminated among yourselves and become judges with evil thoughts?
(James 2:3-4)

While James' teaching above is showing a specific reference to financial favouritism, I think it applies much to us. How often do we start a conversation with someone, "So, Michael, what do you do?" as an occupation? I know that I've found myself guilty of this. And from the side of someone unemployed is, "So, Michael, are you worth my time?"

When a group has been together for a long time, they won't accept an "outsider" in. After the church service, we go out for lunch with the people we know. It's hard to accept this teaching on favouritism, but James 2:9 says, "If you show favoritism, you sin and are convicted by the law as lawbreakers."

I bring up these sins, not to condemn you, but that you may recognize a need for change. I will bring this up more in the following chapter. But, please, with a humble heart, acknowledge God as your standard of "good" and ask Him to give you the Holy Spirit.

Track 11- The 6 O'clock News

In the previous chapter I said, "I bring up these sins, not to condemn you, but that you recognize a need to change." I have also been saying that we shouldn't use the 6 O'clock news as our standard of "good".

A man named John Bradford, who lived in the 1500s, is credited for saying, "There, but for the grace of God, go I." He supposedly would use this saying, for example, when he would walk down the street and see a drunken man stumbling along the road, he'd say, "There, but for the grace of God, goes John Bradford." Another example that I've heard of him saying this was in reference to seeing a man condemned for committing a crime and being taken to jail in chains; "There, but for the grace of God, go I." In either situation, Bradford was right: If not for God's grace, he would be that stumbling man, or the man condemned for a crime.

I bring this up because we watch the 6 O'Clock news and play judge and executioner so easily. The news fills our TVs with the worst of the worst and in comparison, we say, "Wow. I'm a pretty good person." But you are that rapist, you are that murderer, the only reason your face isn't on the TV screen or in the newspaper is because of God's grace. If you're in a European country or North America, your nation was founded on the Word of God. Your standard of "Right and Wrong" or "Good and Evil" is because of God. Sadly, we are removing God out of these nations and think we are all inherently good with no regard for God.

I would recommend reading the book of Judges which is about the exact same thing. After fleeing Egypt where they were slaves and wandering the desert where God gave them the law separating them from other people groups. Finally, Israel would enter the Promised Land ruled by a number of people groups with all sorts of perverted and wicked traditions. Soon, the Israelites would begin to act in the same way as the people around them with no regard for the God who brought them there. And when they find themselves taken captive by these people, again and again, they would cry out to God when they realize how cruel these nations are. God, being merciful, would raise up a judge and the people are freed and find peace. But when that judge dies, the people go back to following their own moral "good".

Now, my point is that if John Bradford were watching the 6 o'clock news, he would say, "If not for the grace of God that would be me." Bradford recognized how much we are in desperate need of the knowledge and grace of God.

By God's mercy and grace, I will see His eternal kingdom. By no means would I see it because

I am "good enough" or try enough. My "Assurance of Salvation" only comes from a growing love for who God is and my willingness to accept correction.

My point in this chapter is that when we watch the 6 o'clock news, it should continue to remind us that we are all fallen people. Not one of us is "good enough" for God. We need to recognize our need for God and his Word, which is the Bible, to be our guide. And when we do sin, which we all do, we need to turn to Jesus Christ.

While I agree with the need for a judicial system, I'm reminded that I am not so "holy" that I alone can judge others. Sadly, in our criticism we think, "If only a conservative government or if only a liberal government… If only this or that…" and on and on. If anything, we should think, "If only people actually knew the God of the Bible and sought after Him."

Apostle Paul tells Timothy to continue in the reading of Scripture and preaching and teaching (1 Timothy 4:13). In his second letter to Timothy, Paul tells Timothy,

> "All Scripture is God-breathed and
> is useful in teaching, rebuking, and training in
> righteousness." (2 Timothy 3:16)

Romans 3:23 says that we have all fallen short of the glory of God. So, until Jesus Christ is placed on his throne in this world, there will always be problems. So, let us say, "There, but for the grace of God, go I."

Track 12- Conclusion

Surely the arm of the LORD is not too short to save,
nor his ear too dull to hear.
But your iniquities have separated
you from your God;
your sins have hidden his face from you,
so that he will not hear. (Isaiah 59:1-2)

As much as you have sinned, "the arm of the LORD is not too short to save…" But understand that it is because of your sins, your standard of "good", that you have been separated from the eternal God and the eternal life that you are created for.

I don't know at what point you are "saved". So, I don't know if there is much more to say on your journey to find "Assurance of Salvation." Believing in Jesus Christ, saying a one-time prayer, is not as "assuring" as getting to know who God is. That's why I shared my story.

I hear people talk about their "Personal Relationship With God" and it bothers me. It bothers me because then we make God in our own image: In my "personal relationship with God", He wants me to have multiple sexual partners; He wants me to divorce my spouse for any reason because God wants me to be happy. Sadly, this is far too common. We abandon the glory of God for the glory of ourselves. What people should discuss is how they personally relate to God. If I believe in the God of the Bible as a Father who guides and counsels me, and another believes in the God who encourages greed, swearing, anger, or selfish ambitions, can we conclude that we believe in a different God?

My point is that my "assurance" does not come from a supernatural experience or from believing that He loves me, to which many accept and simply go off and live their lives. My "assurance" comes from realizing who He is and wants me to love Him in return. And when I realize who God is and I see the 6 o'clock news, I ask God to help me share His message of love, grace, mercy and forgiveness. And I look at my life and think, "How can I use what I have to reach others?"

My "assurance" comes when I feel condemned and realize that Jesus saved me. I consider Nehemiah's prayer in Nehemiah 1:5-11, where he is confessing his need for God, but also acknowledging his sins. Or Ezra's prayer in Ezra 9:6-15, where he confesses his sins, but thanks God for his grace and mercy.

It's not a sin to want eternal life. Ecclesiastes 3:11 tells us that it is God who sets eternity in our hearts. But Hebrews 6 tells us to move on from elementary teachings of faith in Jesus Christ and move on to maturity. Jesus came to set us free from sin and reunite us with God, but I am greatly concerned that most people don't want to address sin in their lives. Can you imagine the horror if a man like Adolf Hitler lived for eternity with an unrepentant heart? There are people in my life who have the same unrepentant heart.

I desperately want you to know God and how good He truly is. He is not a religious figure saying "Do this and don't do that", he is a loving Father trying to guide you. And in getting to know Him, your assurance will become more and more secure.

So, I encourage you to read Exodus, Leviticus and Deuteronomy. Consider reading Psalms and Proverbs. I love Job 38-41 whereas God speaks out to Job and reminds Job of what He, God, has already done in all of creation: This brings Job to realize how small his problems are in light of eternity, even though the problems were the loss of his children.

Please, remember that you are not saved by simply reading the Bible, but through your attitude towards correction and repentance.

No discipline seems pleasant at the time, but painful. Later on, however, it produces a harvest of righteousness and peace for those who have been trained by it. (Hebrews 12:11)